ls

What is the Way of the Wilderness?

Prairiewoods

What is the Way of the Wilderness?

An Introduction to the

Wilderness Way Community

by
Rev. Solveig Nilsen-Goodin
and the Wilderness Way Community

To Contact WILDERNESS WAY
      Website: www.wildernesswaypdx.org
      Email: wildernesswaycommunity@gmail.com
      Facebook: Wilderness Way

Published by

ZION PUBLISHING
Des Moines IA
www.zionpublishing.org

Wilderness Way exists to ground and cultivate "wild" Christian disciples and fearless spiritual leaders, rooted in the natural world and the prophetic Christian tradition, offering our lives for the transformation of our culture and economy into one that Jesus might recognize as what he called the Kingdom of God, what we might call the Ecosystem of God.

from the *Wilderness Way Mission Statement*

Table of Contents

Welcome!

Manna Rebirth

We are ready! We are ready!
We are ready for the manna rebirth!

No more "Big Deals" or profits over people.
We want community where everybody has enough!

We don't need nothing, just our people
And the wisdom that's been with us all this time!

There is life here! Can you feel it moving?
It's the ancient music of the manna rebirth!

We are ready! We are ready!
We are ready for the manna rebirth!

Wilderness Way Community Song
By Nathan Holst

WELCOME

Welcome to this introduction to the Wilderness Way Community! Maybe you picked up this book because you're looking for something like church (but perhaps not like the church you grew up in). Maybe you are longing for some kind of spiritual community with other people who find God in the woods. Maybe you don't identify as Christian but you are intrigued by a community grounded in Christian tradition and also committed to the liberation of everyone. Maybe you are already part of a church but are wondering what questions we have been asking that might inspire courage and creativity in your own community. Maybe you're half way across the country or the world and you've heard about this way of being Christian community and you're wondering what a Wilderness Way Community in your own place might look like. Maybe you're just curious about one of the many ways the Spirit is reforming the church in the 21st century. Or maybe you're a friend or neighbor, family member or coworker of a Wilderness Way member, and you're excited to read more about this thing called Wilderness Way. Whatever your reason for flipping open this book, thank you for honoring us by reading these pages.

This year, 2016, marks Wilderness Way's tenth birthday! To celebrate, we decided to practice Jubilee[1] by compiling and redistributing some of the wisdom we have discovered in our first decade. In this brief introduction to our community you will catch a glimpse of our purpose and passions, our processes and paradoxes. A host of stories and songs, wanderings and wonderings remain beyond the scope of this intro-

---

1 Jubilee is radical sharing. See our "Core Values and Practices" section for more on what Jubilee means to Wilderness Way.

duction, but our hope is that what you read here will inspire you, spark your imaginations, and open up visions for how you and your communities might reform and transform the church, the economy and our culture by walking the Wilderness Way.

The Basics

Come Gather 'Round, My Friends

Come gather 'round, my friends!
Come gather 'round, my friends!
Welcome, everyone, to the wilderness!

Come, you who hunger for freedom!
Come, you who thirst for compassion!
Welcome, everyone, to the wilderness!

Sabbath and jubilee!
Shalom and community!
Welcome, everyone, to the wilderness!

Wilderness Way Community Song
Lyrics by Solveig Nilsen-Goodin
(original tune and lyrics by Ray Makeever,
"Come, Let Us Worship God")

WEEKLY GATHERINGS

Our power and connection as a community grows out of our weekly gatherings. At the time of this printing, we come together most Sundays from 3:00—5:30 p.m. at the Leaven Community Center in Portland, Oregon. The consistent ritual rhythm of each gathering creates a container in which we encounter sacred story in a variety of ways. For a more detailed description, see the "Roots" section.

1st Sundays: Community Autobiographies

2nd Sundays: Liberation Bible Study

3rd Sundays: Hike Sunday (Communal Sabbath Practice): Connecting with the sacred earth and each other with a walk in the woods and community potluck
>   2:00—4:00ish walk
>   4:30—7:30ish potluck, singing, drumming, genuine community hilarity, connection and joy

4th Sundays: The Practices of Sabbath, Jubilee and Shalom

5th Sundays: As the Spirit moves!

(Note: This rhythm does occasionally change due to community events or needs. We post our scheduled changes on our website.)

BRIEF HISTORY AND AFFILIATION

Rev. Solveig Nilsen-Goodin and Mark Douglass first caught the vision of Wilderness Way in the spring of 2006. Although Solveig and Mark were born and bred Lutherans and were leaders within the church, for the first seven years of its life, Wilderness Way took root and developed independent of any denominational affiliation.

Then through a long, winding journey that accidentally included a brief stint as a "corporation" in the eyes of the IRS, Wilderness Way found a place as a "synodically authorized worshiping community of the Oregon Synod of the Evangelical Lutheran Church in America." This designation bears the lovely acronym of SAWC, which we prefer to pronounce "saucy." We are grateful for the partnership of an institutional church eager to support new models of ministry.

CHILDREN OF WILDERNESS WAY

Children contribute vital life energy to Wilderness Way. Filled with passion and potential, they, like the adults, are growing to be courageous spiritual leaders in the world. To support their development, two highly-skilled teachers innovatively work, play and learn with them during the center portion of our Sunday gatherings. Our Children's School includes structured, age-appropriate activities for...

- Deepening children's connection with the sacred earth;
- Practicing the community's "Skills of Loving—seeing, hearing, honoring, responding to needs, having good will" (see the "Trunk" section for more on these Skills of Loving);

- Engaging in developmentally appropriate anti-oppression and collective liberation work;
- Giving and receiving social-emotional support;
- Learning biblical stories that communicate our core values of Sabbath, Jubilee and Shalom.

The Wilderness Way Children's School welcomes not only children whose families are part of our community but also children whose adults are not regular participants in Wilderness Way. Children and adults gather in one group for song and ritual from 3:00—3:30 p.m. and 5:15—5:30 p.m. Children who come only to the school participate from 3:30—5:00 p.m. and are then blessed on their way.

WELCOME STATEMENT

Our community welcomes everyone. Period. We place high value on creating a safe and courageous place for people of all ages, gender identities and expressions, sexual orientations, races, backgrounds, ethnicities, and abilities. We welcome all to be, and to be beloved, exactly as we are. More than that, grounded in the natural world and the prophetic Christian tradition, Wilderness Way calls each of us to grow and to evolve, to be powerful and to be fearless, to bring everything we have and to bring everything we are to our collective pursuit of liberation and abundant life for all.

People of varying gender identities/expressions and sexual orientations continue to be actively excluded from some Christian communities. Many Christian communities categorically exclude women from leadership, regardless of their sexual orientation or gender identity/expression, while others specifically exclude from leadership roles those who do not conform to heteronormative sexual orientations or gender identities/expressions. We wrote and adopted a Statement of Welcome in order to publicly declare our priority—providing a safe and welcoming community for all people. While Wilderness Way is not a Lutheran congregation per se, we are under the institutional umbrella of the Evangelical Lutheran Church in America. Therefore, the specific designation we have is as a Reconciling in Christ community through ReconcilingWorks. ReconcilingWorks advocates for "full welcome, inclusion, and equity for all LGBTQ Lutherans in all aspects of the life of their Church, congregations and communities."

WILDERNESS WAY WELCOMING STATEMENT

Adopted June, 2016

The Wilderness Way Community:

Rewilding Christianity

Subverting Empire

Walking the Way

The Wilderness Way Community is dedicated to liberation from oppression in all its forms. Finding our power and wisdom in the prophetic and liberating Christian tradition and the natural world, we empower all people to become fearless spiritual leaders bringing their God-given gifts to the sacred work of dismantling oppressions, healing from them, and creating life-affirming alternatives to them.

Recognizing that for many people churches themselves have been agents of oppression, we unequivocally welcome all people. We particularly embrace transgender, gender variant, queer, lesbian, gay, bisexual, asexual, intersex, people who are questioning their sexuality, and their allies. Many of us in Wilderness Way are queer and/or trans-identified. We are here to walk this path with you. You are not alone.

As part of our commitment to liberation and unequivocal welcome, we participate as a community in anti-racism, anti-sexism and heterosexism, and other anti-oppression trainings annually.

We practice the **Skills of Loving** by
- Seeing and being seen,
- Hearing and speaking truth,
- Responding to needs and making our needs known,
- Having goodwill for self and others,
- Honoring everyone's experience as well as our own.

You are welcome to show up as you are, as who you are (on your best days and your worst days) and be loved and held in this community. You are welcome whether you are Christian-identified, questioning your faith, in recovery from wounds inflicted by religious trauma, simultaneously receiving nourishment from other faith traditions, or simply on your journey. Be ready to be in a community that says YES to all of who you are, a community that calls you into your power for the work of collective liberation. We look forward to meeting and welcoming you.

What is Wilderness Way?

WHAT DOES WILDERNESS MEAN TO US?

The Way of the Wilderness

The way of the wilderness
Calls in the music now.
The way of the wilderness
Calls out our names.
What is the way of the wilderness?
It calls deeper still.

We call for a life of Sabbath.
Listen to the call.
We call for a life of Jubilee!
Listen to the call.
We call for a life of Shalom.
Listen to the call.

Wilderness Way Community Song
By Nathan Holst

MISSION STATEMENT

The current mission statement of our ever-growing, developing, and evolving community:

"Wilderness Way exists to ground and cultivate 'wild' Christian disciples and fearless spiritual leaders, rooted in the natural world and the prophetic Christian tradition, offering our lives for the transformation of our culture and economy into one that Jesus might recognize as what he called the Kingdom of God, what we might call the Ecosystem of God."

Why "wild" Christian disciples? Why fearless spiritual leaders? We are living in an extraordinary time—a moment of profound import in human history. The interlocking crises facing humanity—ecological and economic, political and social, moral and spiritual—have the earth, the children, and those who have been rendered invisible crying out for ordinary people who can remain grounded in their communities, clear about their vision, compassionate toward all people, and courageous in the face of obstacles, while living in highly fearful and anxious times. Our mission emerged in response to precisely this historical moment. So everything we do is in the service of raising up such ordinary leaders.

True as that may be, it also sounds a little grandiose, because, in a funny way, Wilderness Way functions sort of like a traditional church. We come together weekly to be spiritually grounded, challenged, known, loved, and called to our fullest selves for a larger purpose. We are then sent out with that grounding and power to do our work in the world.

Yet there is a significant difference. In Wilderness Way we acknowledge that stories and systems of domination consistently shape and domesticate, privilege and oppress us in complex and unequal ways. These systems perpetuate injustice and inequality and lead us ever deeper into crisis. And though painful to admit, we are complicit in these systems.

Therefore, our ministry in this context is unmasking those systems of oppression, entering the struggles to dismantle them, seeing with new eyes what else is possible, and drawing others toward it with tender urgency.

What is possible? "Enough for everyone!" We sing these words each week as we prepare to celebrate communion.

What is possible? A world in which everyone does have enough. A world of Sabbath, Jubilee, and Shalom.

- Jesus called it the Kingdom of God.

- Martin Luther King, Jr. called it the Beloved Community.

- Dan Erlander calls it the Manna Society.

- Elisabeth Schüssler Fiorenza calls it the Discipleship of Equals and the Commonwealth of G*d.

- Randy Woodley calls it the Community of Creation.

- We are beginning to call it the Ecosystem of God.[1]

---

1 For more on these visions, see *A Testament of Hope: The Essential Writings and Speeches of Martin Luther King Jr.,* edited by James M. Washington; *Manna and Mercy,* by Dan Erlander; *Discipleship of Equals,* and *Jesus: Miriam's Child, Sophia's Prophet,* by Elisabeth Schüssler Fiorenza; and *Shalom and the Community of Creation,* by Randy Woodley.

We walk the Wilderness Way energized and emboldened by such visions, convinced beyond all evidence to the contrary that, in the words of Indian activist, Arundhati Roy, "Another world is not only possible, she is on her way. On a quiet day, I can hear her breathing."[2]

WILDERNESS
Liberating, Prophetic Christian Tradition and Natural World

At Wilderness Way we come together to open up an alternative space within the context of the American empire—a bastion of global capitalism and neocolonialism. We come together to imagine this alternative space as a "wilderness" space, a space in which we can push back the logic of empire and find power in community to imagine and create a new reality; a space in which we can be formed and transformed, forgiven and challenged, untamed and undomesticated.

The wilderness motif runs deep through the whole of scripture. In this motif we discover that at its core, wilderness refers to the places that empire has not been able to control. This is why prophets often come out of the wilderness, and why people seeking liberation from empire go into the wilderness.

Two of the many biblical wilderness stories that shape our imagination are the 40-year Exodus journey of liberation in the wilderness, and Jesus' 40-day wilderness preparation to fulfill his baptismal call.

---

2 See Arundhati Roy's speech at the World Social Forum, 2003.

The Exodus journey of liberation is a powerful prototypical story of a community seeking and attaining its own liberation and then having the dual blessing and challenge of unlearning the worldview of empire and slavery, and reimagining a way of life in harmony with the God of creation and liberation. Carving out "wilderness" spaces invites us also to unlearn the distorted worldviews that have shaped us and to reimagine life in harmony with the God of creation and liberation.

In the same way, Jesus' 40-day wilderness sojourn invites us to take our own call to spiritual leadership seriously. Friend and mentor of Wilderness Way, Ched Myers, describes wilderness sojourns, like the one Jesus took, as "both a very real exterior adventure beyond the margins of society and an interior passage of cleansing….a sojourn through mythic time, in order to encounter the story and destiny of one's self and one's people."[3]

In those 40 days in the wilderness—a space the Roman empire had not completely domesticated—Jesus wrestled deeply with "the Adversary" and the temptations of imperial culture. He grappled with the story of his people and his own place in the world, with his identity and with his baptismal call.

Likewise, in order to develop as courageous spiritual leaders in our time, we also need to find "wilderness" spaces—inside and outside—spaces in which we can wrestle deeply with our own "demons" and the temptations of capitalist, consumer and colonial culture; spaces in which we can come face to

---

3 Myers, Ched, "Led by the Spirit into the Wilderness: Reflections on Lent, Jesus' Temptations and Indigeneity," 2002.

face with the story of our peoples and our varied experiences of privilege and marginalization; spaces in which we can grapple with our own identities and with our own call.

Wilderness, however, is not simply a metaphor or a motif, an imaginative place or space. Every biblical story and every imaginative "wilderness" space we create takes place somewhere: In a particular ecosystem with its particular flora and fauna. In a particular watershed with its particular story of humans and their relationships to the land. In a particular bioregion with its particular history of human interactions, both harmonious and hostile, benevolent and brutal.

Wilderness Way, for example, which finds its home in the Willamette and Columbia River watersheds, currently meets just miles from a portion of the Willamette River declared a Superfund site. This land, once a vibrant trading area for indigenous peoples, was ceded in 1855 by the Kalapuya, Molala, Clackamas and other peoples only after violence and epidemics had devastated over 95 percent of their populations.

Without an intimate connection with place, we easily spiritualize or see only the metaphoric meaning of a thing. For example, when Jesus compels his listeners to pay attention to the birds of the air and the flowers of the field, he calls them not to a greeting-card moment but rather to a radical teaching on how God's intended economy functions. Or how often, for example, do we hear the biblical phrase "living water" solely as metaphor while toxins flow unimpeded into water in countless rivers and oceans, poisoning the water that is the source and substance of life for us and myriad plants and animals—literally, our living water?

Wilderness, therefore, also calls our attention to the earth, the land, the waters, the ecosystems, the biosphere in which we live, imploring us to learn their wisdom, their stories and the ways they have been impacted by empire. The climate crisis facing humanity reveals how deeply so many of us are disconnected from the ecosystems in which we live. Wilderness Way understands that reconnecting with the earth and earth's stories, with wilderness and our own wildness, is not only essential for our healing and survival, it is inevitable for those who seek to follow in the way of Jesus and the untamable, undomesticatable God of Life.

The breadth and depth of these meanings of wilderness have revealed to us what we call the Wilderness Way: the way of Sabbath, Jubilee and Shalom.

CORE VALUES AND PRACTICES
Sabbath, Jubilee and Shalom

Sabbath, Jubilee and Shalom are foundational biblical wisdom, rooted in the Exodus story and manifest also in the Jesus story. In his article, "Where Post-Colonial and Pre-Colonial Thought Touch Jesus," friend of Wilderness Way, Randy Woodley, says this: "The core of Jesus' thought was developed from an ancient egalitarian-based, Shalom-Sabbath-Jubilee system... [that] emphasized empowering the marginalized and correcting societal injustice."[4] These three words—Sabbath, Jubilee, Shalom—reflect to us the heart of "natural" and divine Sophia-Wisdom, the heart of Jesus' ministry and truly the Way of Life.

Desiring to reanimate this ancient system for our time and place, we listened for the essence of Sabbath, Jubilee and Shalom and sought words to express that wisdom in our context. How we defined those words ten years ago still challenges and focuses our process of undomestication and collective liberation. This is the Wilderness Way.

---

4 Woodley, Randy, "Where Post-Colonial and Pre-Colonial Thought Touch Jesus," *Geez Magazine*, Fall 2015, page 15. Randy and his wife, Edith, are actively nurturing Eloheh (ay-luh-hay) Farm – a farm, community and school in Newberg, Oregon, whose goal is to cooperate with all creation and create a model farm for an abundant future.

Sabbath

Resisting the pressure to incessantly "do" and "produce" by re-grounding oneself in the beauty, abundance and trust-worthiness of the sacred universe, in order to:

- Restore balance to self and relationships,
- Remember who we are and why we are here, and
- Rekindle creativity and passion for life.

Jubilee

Redefining how much is enough in a hyper-consumer society, in order to:

- Restore value to life and relationships in a capitalistic economy,
- Release ourselves and others from the burdens of debt, wealth or poverty, and
- Reduce the negative ecological impact of our lives on the planet.

Shalom

Recognizing the inherent wholeness and unity of all creation, in order to:

- Restore the birthright of all people to live without violence and to be treated with dignity,
- Reestablish relationships of forgiveness and healing with others, including the earth and those who may be considered our "enemies," and
- Recreate continually the conditions for peace in the midst of world cultures obsessed with war.

WILDERNESS WAY: A CHRISTIAN COMMUNITY, BUT NOT ONLY FOR CHRISTIANS

Wilderness Way is a Christian community. We will get to what that means, but first we need to say a little about what that does not mean. Being an explicitly Christian community does not mean that everyone walking the Wilderness Way calls themselves a Christian. Some can hardly stomach the word. And not without good reason. In fact, most of us who do identify ourselves as Christian find ourselves putting any number of qualifiers on the word because there are so many historical and present examples of exclusion, abuse and brutality at the hands of Christians or Christian institutions. This reality grieves us, but we face it squarely, acknowledging both the oppressive and the liberating strands of this faith tradition, and claiming the liberating strands as our source of power and life.

Identifying ourselves as a Christian community also does not mean we claim that Christianity is superior to and therefore exclusive of other faith traditions. Truth be told, most of us in Wilderness Way have explored or currently draw wisdom and life from a variety of other spiritual traditions. These experiences and perspectives enrich our community tremendously and we honor them.

At the very same time, many of us are already or are becoming deeply committed to Christian faith as we access its power and wisdom through scripture, story, song, sacrament, and engaging our core practices. What draws each of us deeper into Christian faith varies widely.

Some are compelled by the scriptural stories—stories that provide a counter-narrative to destructive cultural stories that shape our lives, while others hear the call to follow the way of costly discipleship and empire-defying resurrection.

For some Christ is experienced as a community of radical acceptance and the power of love, forgiveness, reconciliation and healing. For others, the divine is revealed in the practices of Sabbath, Jubilee and Shalom—practices that resonate with the deep values of many traditions.

Some devote themselves to a personal or mystical relationship with Jesus, while others seek and find Christ in the community itself. Still others struggle with the figure of Jesus.

But as a Christian community, we root ourselves in and draw life as a community from what we find to be the most liberating and prophetic wisdom, power, stories and rituals of the Christian tradition, and from creation (the first "Word" of God) manifest in our watersheds. We do this while holding the value of honoring everyone's right to think and feel as they do about Christianity, Jesus, prayer, sacraments, everything.

Our goal is not to lead people to a shared belief about who Jesus is or was, why he died or what his death means, whether the resurrection actually happened or whether it is a metaphor. Nor is it to arrive at some common experience of grace or the Gospel or the "Word" or the cross, or whatever language speaks of the heart of Christianity for some of us. We simply and explicitly create space, space where people can encounter the wild and untamable, healing and liberating God of Jesus through scripture, sacrament, nature, prayer, community, story, song, and practice. And together we dare to trust Her/Them/Him to deconstruct, undomesticate, heal, transform and love us into fearless spiritual leaders dedicated to manifesting Sabbath, Jubilee and Shalom as:

the Kingdom of God,
  the Beloved Community,
    the Manna Society,
      the Discipleship of Equals,
        the Commonwealth of G*d,
          the Community of Creation,
            the Ecosystem of God—in our own time and place.

SOME OF THE WAYS WE DESCRIBE WILDERNESS WAY

Describing Wilderness Way to others is not a simple task. The intent of this book is to illuminate the grounding places and some of the inner workings of the community, but each Wilderness Way member's experience is unique. The descriptions below reflect some of the ways our children and adults talk to others about their experience in Wilderness Way.

"How I usually explain Wilderness Way (an unglamorous but totally honest account):

NEWER FRIEND: Want to go for a hike on Sunday?

ME: What's your time-frame like?

FRIEND: I was thinking of leaving around 11 or 12:00.

ME: Well...I have Wilderness Way in the afternoon on Sundays, at 3:00.

FRIEND: [quizzical face]

ME: Wilderness Way is my tree church community.

FRIEND: Say more!

ME: Well, it's a smallish group of folks who talk about rooting ourselves with one foot in the nature story and one foot in the Jesus story. Drawing from those two places doesn't cover all of my spiritual ground, but the community is expansive enough for me to hold my relatively wide spectrum beliefs and still participate whole heartedly, so that works. We meet outside when we can, and we hike and have a potluck on the third Sundays. The other Sundays each have their own rhythms. My favorite is the autobiography Sunday, when one person at a time shares in depth about an aspect of their life. We also sing a lot. They're my people. I love them. It's awesome.

FRIEND: It sounds awesome!

ME: Yep. So, I usually try to get an early start on Sunday adventures, to be back by 3:00.

FRIEND: That's cool."

"It is a spiritual community where all are welcome, no matter what you believe. We are grounded in values and practices that promote both personal and collective liberation and deep connection to nature and natural rhythms. We are both informed by and seek to heal Christianity and remind ourselves and others what it means to be children of God in today's world."

"Wilderness Way is a homecoming, a call to action, and a ceremony. It is a spiritual community where we ground ourselves in tradition, ritual, skills of loving, and internal and external wilderness practices in order to build the Beloved Community."

"One of the many strengths of Wilderness Way is that it is primarily a community of shared practices, rather than having specific shared beliefs. This allows for collaboration, accountability, and growth in areas of spiritual practice, social action, and integrated life, while honoring diverse beliefs and each individual's strengths and unique ways of being/ knowing/exploring a life of wild and radical discipleship and faithfulness."

"Wilderness Way is a play place to have fun and connect to the wilderness."

"Wilderness Way is an expansive and open group of people and practices where I get encouragement, inspiration, guidance and nourishment to grow spiritually. It's where I am fed so I can seek God and do the work in the world that I am called to do. It's a place where I am encouraged to adventurously and authentically call upon the powers that be to do things I didn't think possible. It's where I learn about the Jesus who defied the state and community sanctioned violence and exploitation and had radical ideas of who was acceptable and beloved. As a Queer ecofeminist and generally unconventional person I found a home. It's a home where I am not pigeonholed into one type of faith but I am given opportunities to take my faith to the streets. It's a place where organizers and activists meet to send our roots back into the dirt and drink deeply of the Earth/God-given sanity. It's where we can remember why and how we strive for peace and justice."

"Wilderness Way is like doing mushrooms and the Occupy movement combined!"

"Wilderness Way is extremely hard to describe! Its depth and breadth are beyond category, but I would use the following words to offer a "glimpse" of what it is about: rewilding, nature-connection, people-connection, ritual, space for grief, deconstructing empire, subversive, open, joy-filled, full of aunties and uncles for our young ones."

"Wilderness Way is a loving community that helps people get in touch with the wilderness."

"Wilderness Way is a new expression of religion wholesale. It is a space for those who have grown restless in the church, those who find the spiritual practices of dominant Christianity banal. Upon entering the church I always remove the "implements of empire." That is to say I remove my wallet, my cell phone (if I didn't lose it recently) and my shoes. I do these same things every time I enter my house, but in this context the actions are symbols. The removal of these items from myself is the action of removing myself from the dominant society. The main body of each time together is the liminal space we use to create and live out the imagined narrative we would like to bring to reality. Not only do our Wilderness Way rituals help change behavior and worldview over time, but they can also create alternative future realities that would not otherwise have been realized."

Wilderness Way

THE COMMUNITY AS A TREE

I Want to Be Alive!

We seek wisdom from the trees,
From the stories of Jesus, of you and of me.
We seek wisdom from the bees,
From the practice of Sabbath, Shalom and Jubilee!
'Cuz this is life. This is life!
And I want to be alive for it!
I want to be alive!

Wilderness Way Community Song
By Solveig Nilsen-Goodin

OUR COMMUNITY METAPHOR

Metaphors matter. The ways we think about church matter. The language we use to describe our faith communities matters. If we see the church as a hospital for the sick, a refuge against the problems of life, a social club, a family, or (in more traditional language) a fortress, an army, a servant-church, the body of Christ, that metaphor will shape what we do and don't do, who is welcome and who isn't, what we can imagine and what we can't.

Grounded in the natural world as well as the prophetic Christian tradition, the metaphor of Wilderness opens up new possibilities for how we structure and imagine ourselves as Christian community. Where many churches have adopted corporate structural models, we remain rooted in our watersheds and our wilderness metaphor, imagining ourselves rather as a community modeled on the organizational wisdom of a tree.

The seed of Wilderness Way was planted in the imaginations of two visionaries. They gathered a small community, and together this community transplanted the seedling into the holy ground of wilderness—liberative scripture, the natural world and their shared wisdom of Sabbath, Jubilee and Shalom. The roots held and deepened, and the tree grew. Now, ten years later, Wilderness Way is thriving. Planted within an emerging forest of cross-pollinating partners (faith-based and non-faith-based), we mutually nourish and strengthen one another as we slowly grow into what will, we hope, one day be a rich and diverse, wise and sacred old growth forest of faith and life.

As members of the Wilderness Way Community, we have two roles. We are part of the tree (the leaves in this metaphor), and we are also those who tend the tree. There have been times for pruning ideas or visions, but mostly we who tend this tree honor it best by watching, listening, and paying attention, learning and discovering what it wants to be, what fruit it wants to bear, how deep and broad its root structure wants to extend, how its bark and trunk will develop, how big it will grow and how many seeds it will scatter. We do this because Wilderness Way is its own being, is its own particular species, with its own spirit and integrity. The seed was planted for the very times in which we are living. Watching and tending, we discover what new life it brings into the world.

Of course, every metaphor has elements that don't quite work, but the metaphor of a tree makes sense to us, and it reminds us regularly that Wilderness Way is much more than our own personal experience of it. Each part of this metaphor—this tree-community—has meaning and opens our eyes to see the miracle that it is.

SEED, SUN, SOIL, AIR, WATER
The Great Economy of Grace

We can't talk about who we are as a faith community without first acknowledging that everything we have become, everything we are, everything we ever will be is all a gift of grace. A tree—like a person, like every created being—is the manifestation of sun, air, water, nutrients, and a miraculous spirit/essence-bearing seed that becomes the unique individual within a species that it is. But the tree, like the person, did not create itself. Its very existence is a gift, as is every moment it continues to draw life from the elements and from the Spirit.

So too the Wilderness Way Community did not create itself. Yes, it has been nurtured along the way by faithful tending. But like early Christian leaders Phoebe and Junia, Paul and Apollos, we acknowledge that though we plant and water our tree-communities, "God gives the growth." (1 Cor. 3:7b) Everything is a gift. Everything. Everything we are, everything we have, everything we (think we) own.

Recognizing the gift: that's where it all begins.

ROOTS
Our Sunday and Monthly Rhythms

A radical economy undergirds the forest. Radical, from the Latin "*radix*," means "root." The roots of Wilderness Way keep a radical trajectory alive in our community. Much of the biomass of the forest lives underground—out of sight, but essential to the life above. In this underground matrix, bugs, roots, worms, mycelium, microscopic organisms and animals make life together by exchanging resources. In this active economy inhabiting the soil under our feet, roots accomplish two main purposes.

First, they provide structural support for the weight of the tree and bulwark against the forces of weather that buffet the leaves. To rise up, a plant must first strongly root down. So too do our weekly gatherings anchor our members in the stable soil of the economy of grace.

Second, roots seek out the nutrients and water necessary for growth. While carbon, freely available in the air, composes most of the structure of the tree, nitrogen, phosphorus and potassium compounds create the living molecules in the matrix of the tree. Our weekly gatherings help us tap into the nourishing traditions of Sabbath, Shalom, and Jubilee that keep our community dynamic, healthy, and strong.

Finally, roots and leaves live in a dynamic relationship. As roots find nutrients and water, the trunk pumps these up to feed the growth of the leaves above, while at the same time the leaves utilize the energy of the sun to provide energy for the tireless work of roots seeking out sustenance and hydration. In the same way, our gatherings nourish the lives of our members, while our members also animate our gatherings with their life-energy. "If our roots aren't strong, the leaves are the first to go," said one of our members (the leaves being the people that make up Wilderness Way). So we tend to our roots.

The two primary characteristics of our gatherings are the Sunday rhythm and our monthly rhythm.

Our Sunday Rhythm—The Liturgy of Liberation

Our Liturgy of Liberation has three main parts, corresponding both to the Exodus journey of liberation and to the journey of discipleship. As such this Liturgy of Liberation is a weekly rite of passage, reanimating these ancient stories in our own time and place, so our stories might also become stories of liberation and discipleship.

PART I: PASSING THROUGH THE WATERS. Here, singing and shoeless, standing on holy ground, we anoint ourselves with water, leaving behind the ways of domination, and we claim anew the ways of liberation. Here we also acknowledge that though the water may symbolize the Red Sea of the Exodus or the Jordan River of Jesus' baptism, our water—this living water—flows from the Bull Run watershed on Mt. Hood (or, *Wy'East,* as the mountain was known before colonization), and so our liberation is quite literally and intimately connected with the liberation of this water.

PART II: "WILDERNESS" TIME. During this time we practice discipleship by learning and relearning the ancient wisdom—how to live free as sacred beings, how to live in community with all that is, and how to live in abundance where there is enough for everyone. As we relearn the ancient wisdom, we also have to unlearn internalized messages and patterns of oppression shaped by the logic of empire. And so this "wilderness" time is also a time of deconstruction and reconstruction, a time of disillusionment and discovery, a time of grappling with sacred stories and uncovering power in our own stories, a time of connecting with the God of Life and listening to the call of that God on our lives.

PART III: CELEBRATION AND COMMITMENT. We celebrate communion singing, "Enough for Everyone!" In the spirit of our biblical ancestors who shared manna in the wilderness, we participate in God's divine economy of grace by feeding one another, making sure all are fed.[1] And in memory of the last meal Jesus shared with the disciples the night before his execution, we receive the gift and reaffirm our commitment to the Wilderness Way, to the practice of Sabbath, Jubilee and Shalom, to Jesus' vision of the Kingdom—the Ecosystem—of God.

Our Monthly Rhythm

Our gatherings feel creative and energetic because the second part of our liturgy, the "wilderness" time described above, is different every Sunday. Each week, in a consistent rhythm, we seek to encounter the wisdom and power of the God of Life—the living "Word" of God—as it manifests in our stories, in scripture, in nature and in the practice of Sabbath, Jubilee and Shalom.

On the first Sundays of the month we learn from each other's deep wisdom as members share a piece of their autobiographies. We currently cycle through spiritual, money and nature autobiographies, telling our stories to share experiences of hardships and privilege and to uncover hidden connections, power and wisdom we did not know we had. By shining light on the often unexplored parts of our stories,

---

1 At the time of this publication, we share juice (sometimes we even have juice from berries we have picked and canned ourselves!) and tortillas or rice crackers. These choices were made in response to expressed needs within the community. As needs change, our practice will change too. As with all aspects of Wilderness Way, each person is welcome to participate or not but no one is ever excluded.

we grow in our ability to create new narratives for ourselves and our communities.

On the second Sundays of the month we practice "liberation Bible study," diving into scripture and seeking the deep wisdom, power and liberation embedded in these ancient stories of our lineage of faith. Our Bible studies combine vulnerable conversation, scholarly insight, and collective critical reflection on our society, our lives and the texts themselves. Some of our much-loved and used resources and guides are:

> *The Inclusive Bible: The First Egalitarian Translation,* by Priests for Equality;
> *The Biblical Vision of Sabbath Economics,* by Ched Myers;
> *Manna and Mercy,* by Rev. Dan Erlander;
> The opening of Leslie Marmon Silko's novel, *Ceremony.*

On the third Sundays of the month we break from this pattern to take our Sabbath walk and share a meal together—immersing ourselves in the wisdom of our own sacred watershed. Our current practice is to walk at the same location every month in order to get to know it well and recognize its changes throughout the seasons. We often begin by reading together the Chinook Blessing Litany.[2] Typically we walk and talk, connecting with each other and place. Then, at the center of our walk, we find a "sit spot," drop into silence and enter more deeply into communion with the life of this watershed. We regather to share our experiences. This is a simple yet profound practice. We don't bring the "holy things" into the wilderness, we encounter the holy in the wilderness.

---

2 "Chinook Blessing Litany," in *Earth Prayers: 365 Prayers, Poems, and Invocations from Around the World,* Elizabeth Roberts and Elias Amidon, eds. New York, NY: HarperCollins Publishers, 1991, p. 106-107

On the fourth Sundays we focus on practice. How are we practicing our core values of Sabbath, Jubilee, and Shalom? What is the cost of this kind of discipleship? How can we support one another to continue walking the Wilderness Way and to grow in our public leadership? On this Sunday, we often talk about building a culture of loving accountability as we struggle and strive to live out the values we claim.

TRUNK
Our Structure and Culture, the Tensions We Hold

The trunk of a tree provides its structure. Without the formation of trunks bolstered by rigid compounds like lignin and cellulose, plants could not reach up toward the energy of the sun. Tree trunks support the leaf matter at the top and protect the inner "heartwood" of the tree that transports nutrients up and down the tree. Have you ever watched a tree grow? You may have noticed that new woody growth is green and soft in the first year, but hardens to become brown and sturdy by the next year. Thus new growth is flexible, but as the growth continues, it becomes more hardy and stable to continue further growth. Further, as the tree grows up, the bark grows outward, so that only the structural support that is needed for new growth is formed, and no more.

Understanding that the purpose of structure is principally to support health and new growth, we keep our structure to a minimum in Wilderness Way, maintaining just enough structure to undergird a culture of loving relationships and courageous action. Some of our woody structures are soft and flexible, supporting new ideas or projects. Other structures have been around much longer and have grown into the thick trunk that holds our entire community.

Here are a few things we know about our structure and our culture (among the many things we do not yet know).

Structure

Membership. Who is a member of Wilderness Way? The word "member" doesn't exactly work for us, but we have not come up with anything better at this point. Traditional membership criteria for churches (baptism and/or confirmation) also don't really work because we aren't insistent that full community participants self-identify as Christian. So what does membership mean for Wilderness Way?

We are still figuring this out, but perhaps the best analogy for how we understand membership would be that Wilderness Way is similar to a 12-Step group. In 12-Step groups, the only membership criteria is a desire for recovery. So too, each person's desire to be in community with others seeking to walk the Wilderness Way is itself the only criteria for membership at this point.

12-Step groups are also clear that in the meetings the literature, traditions and sharing all come from the recovery movement. While many members of 12-Step groups also have therapists, faith traditions and other support systems, when they come to a meeting, they draw on the wisdom and power of the 12-Step movement. In the same way, while most individual members of Wilderness Way have other support systems and even other faith traditions they claim, when we gather as a community we are explicitly accessing the wisdom and power of nature and the radical/prophetic/liberative Christian tradition and practicing the ways of Sabbath, Jubilee and Shalom.

On a functional level, membership actually sorts itself out pretty easily. The most accurate indication we have of membership is this: If you come to the weekly gatherings whenever you can, and if you choose to be on the very active email list that we use for every manner of communication, from babysitting requests and dance party invitations to calls for prayer and participation in protests, then God bless you, you're an active member of Wilderness Way. And beyond that, if you want to be on the equally active group text list? You're definitely in.

In terms of contributions of time and money to support the community, we don't currently have a standard expectation. However, we are beginning to experiment with an annual ritual of cost- and time-sharing in which each person is invited to discern and share (using a process that feels right for our community) how much time and money they are able to contribute to the mutual life of the community for the coming year. This is still in process.

We currently have three paid leaders: one part-time pastor/developer, and two very part-time children's teachers. Financial compensation allows them to have protected time to focus their energy on nurturing the vision and development of the community. We have a council that meets monthly to actively participate in this nurturing and development work.

Right now, we have no terms or particular criteria for council membership except that all are active members of Wilderness Way and are willing and wanting to commit time and energy to the council's work. These meetings are always open to everyone in the community who wishes to attend. Besides that, they always happen in someone's home, with a potluck and much hilarity.

Culture

The culture of Wilderness Way is perhaps best characterized by the Skills of Loving[3] (part of our larger Shalom Covenant). These five Skills of Loving are:

- SEEING others in their uniqueness, not how we want or assume them to be, and allowing ourselves to be seen,
- HEARING what others are truly saying, not what we wish they were saying, as well as speaking our own truth with kindness and respect,
- HONORING others' feelings and ideas, recognizing others' right to think and feel as they do, as well as our own,
- CHOOSING to have good will for others and self, regardless of differences or difficulties, and
- RESPONDING to needs and "being there" for others, within the limits of our value systems, when those needs are made known; as well as taking the responsibility to make our needs known.

We recommit to practicing these Skills of Loving as we begin each "wilderness" section of our gatherings. We read them aloud and share stories about how they are shaping our lives. These practices help us create a loving and courageous container in which each of us can be vulnerable, fall apart, fail miserably at the very skills we seek to practice, and also to be held, to be beheld and to be called to our higher selves.

---

3 These five Skills of Loving originated with Jerry Jud, founder of Shalom Mountain Retreat Center in Livingston Manor, NY, along with Elisabeth Jud. The Principles and Skills of Loving remain central to the life and practice of Shalom Mountain. The original Skills of Loving have been adapted slightly for use within our community.

The Tensions We Hold

As the culture of the community has evolved, we have happened upon many situations in which two values seem to be at odds with each other. As much as we can, we try to name and hold these dichotomies in creative and loving tension.

Some of the many both/ands we hold:

—informality/playfulness

—accountability/transparency

—capital

—creating means of support outside of capitalism

—time and energy going into the community

—directing our time and energy out into the world

—strong internal relationships

—openness to newcomers

—acting publicly for justice together on short notice if needed

—communal participation in decision-making

—sharing and developing leadership

—skilled and paid leadership

Other tensions come and go, but all healthy tensions stimulate maturation, so we hold them with gratitude and goodwill.

IMBALANCES AND DISEASES
Potential Susceptibilities

Farmers and orchardists have been fighting disease for a long time. But where the industrial model of pest and disease control has a war mentality of carpet-bombing any threat, a more sound paradigm for crop management follows principles such as these:

- healthy plants can fight off pests and disease better than unhealthy plants;
- particular pests or diseases should be identified and responded to specifically, rather than preemptively spraying with toxic chemicals that may not even be necessary;
- treatments are specific to the disease or pest you are facing;
- and finally, diversity makes for healthier systems than monocultures.

This analogy relates easily to communities. By being aware of our weaknesses to disease and our tendencies to get out of balance, we seek to nurture a healthy, diverse community—a community resilient in the face of dangers to our common welfare and responsive to the needs present in each source of conflict.

So what are the particular imbalances or diseases to which Wilderness Way is susceptible? There are certainly many we cannot yet see (such is the nature of imbalance and disease), but we are aware of some.

As a community seeking to hold many values in creative tension, we are obviously susceptible to falling too heavily on one side or the other. For example, we could be so focused on outward action that we neglect the work of tending to the community's infrastructure. Or we could be so focused on our internal relationships that we unconsciously send the message that we are not open to new people.

Likewise, as a community that identifies itself explicitly as Christian, but also does not insist that individuals within the community take on that identity for themselves, we could stress one side or the other, forgetting that the both/and lends integrity and power to who we are.

Additionally, as a fairly small community at this point, we have tremendous diversity around gender identity but other areas of diversity are currently less developed. Likewise, our clarity about Wilderness Way being a way of liberation is a strength, but it may also put us at risk of groupthink and attracting people only along ideological lines. These imbalances could create a kind of "monoculture" that weakens our whole tree-community.

So we tend to the tree the best we can, holding one another in loving accountability and remaining open and vulnerable with each other, utilizing our Skills of Loving to identify weaknesses and addressing issues as they arise, welcoming possibilities beyond our limited imaginations and recognizing that we are always evolving. And through it all, remembering the words of one of our favorite songs by Nathan Holst, "Everything I need is right in front of me!"

SYMBIOTIC RELATIONSHIPS
Partners and Co-Conspirators

No single species can exist in isolation. Trees of the forest and savannah depend upon a host of other organisms, including their own species. Underground mycelium conspire with trees to mine nutrients, trading valuable sugars that the trees produce in exchange for nutrients. Fungal partners also connect roots of the same and different species. Through these mycelial networks, "mother trees" help nurse younger ones to good health. Researchers have even documented exchanges between trees of different species mediated by fungus!

In the same way, Wilderness Way benefits profoundly from its relationship with partners and co-conspirators. Sometimes we talk about the Holy Spirit as a mycelium connecting us with so many partners and resources through her mysterious threads of connection!

Trees also benefit from insect allies that pollinate their flowers to produce tasty fruit. With cross-pollination comes resilience, as genetic material is mixed and the seeds have a larger bank of genetic resource from which to draw. Here are some of the many organizations that cross-pollinate with Wilderness Way in various ways. We are stronger, healthier, wiser and more powerful because of our relationships, and for this we give thanks.

Some of our beloved fungal, mycelial and cross-pollinating partners are:

- Bartimaeus Cooperative Ministries, the Radical Discipleship network, and the Watershed Discipleship Alliance
- Beyond Fossil Fuels (an initiative of EcoFaith Recovery)
- EcoFaith Recovery
- Eight Shields: Nature Connection Community
- Eloheh Farm and School
- Leaven Community/Salt and Light Lutheran Church
- Oregon Synod/ELCA
- Peace Church of the Brethren
- SURJ: Showing Up for Racial Justice—PDX Chapter

FRUIT
The Gifts We Give, Work We Do, Dreams We Have

For apple and pear, quince and peach trees, bearing fruit is not just about producing a tasty treat. Bearing fruit is how those trees have decided to share themselves with the world. In the same way, we share ourselves with the world through the "fruit" of our community. To do this we maintain strong symbiotic relationships with partners and cross-pollinators. We also do everything we can to make sure our fruit is healthy and nourished by our roots, and that our fruit is free of diseases.

Additionally, as too much fruit can be too heavy and damage trees without a sturdy trunk or branch, we also try to make sure that we have the structures in place to support our blossoming dreams as they turn into fruit. Fruit trees naturally drop some of their fruit in early summer, as a way to reduce stress on the tree. Similarly, we recognize that as we dream many dreams, it is okay for some of those to drop off if it is not time for them to mature into fruit. Wilderness Way is an odd sort of tree. At any given time, we tend to have some fruit that is maturing, some blossoms developing, and some immature fruit dropping off.

Currently, two of the most delicious fruits Wilderness Way has produced relate to our Children's School. By making the decision to hire two highly skilled teachers (even when, at that point, we only had three children in our community!), we have been able to create a uniquely Wilderness Way-style Children's School that is, in age-appropriate ways, grounding and cultivating "wild" Christian disciples and courageous spiritual leaders. Through a partnership with Beyond Fossil Fuels, for example, three of those fearless spiritual leaders (ages 7—10) called the governor of Oregon to ask her to stop the construction of a liquefied natural gas terminal in Oregon!

In addition, during the summer of 2016, our two teachers launched our first three weeks of Wilderness Way Adventure Camps. With the help of a grant from the Oregon Synod-ELCA, these camps were designed to deepen children's connection with themselves, each other, and the sacred earth, through structured and unstructured activities, developmentally-appropriate anti-oppression and collective liberation work, as well as social and emotional support and development in a play-based curriculum.

We have borne other kinds of fruit as well.

- We offered our collective public leadership in two climate justice actions in partnership with EcoFaith Recovery.

- We are creating and offering public grief rituals at the Leaven Community Center. In partnership with EcoFaith Recovery, we have also created and regularly offer "The River's Lament," a grief ritual telling the story of the Willamette River. The River's Lament has become a model for others around the country seeking to tell the sacred stories of their own rivers and watersheds.

- We are recording and sharing dozens of songs for community singing.

- And we have written the book you are holding in your hands, sharing what we have learned and (we hope!) inspiring the creation of new ways of being church.

Buds and blossoms? We have lots of them! Some of us dream of land to farm, a tiny house village, a yurt for our gatherings, a school for leadership development. Which will mature into fruit? We can't wait to find out!

LEAVES
The Wild Ones of Wilderness Way

"On either side of the river grew the trees of life...their leaves serve as medicine to heal the nations." (Revelation 22:2)

Other than its fruit, leaves are often the most distinctive part of a tree. Oaks, maples and pines, for example, are easily distinguished by a glance at their leaves on the tree or on the ground. Leaves function like little solar panels, catching and collecting those fleeting photons of energy to send down to trunk and roots. All the while, roots are tirelessly mining nutrients in the soil to send up to the leaves.

In Wilderness Way, our people harvest the Light of Life to both feed the community and "heal the nations." In a beautiful expression of interdependence, each member brings energy to the community and at the same time is nourished by the community for their healing work in the world. Collectively and in countless ordinary and unique, small and big ways, we offer ourselves for the inward and outward work of healing and restoring the beloved Ecosystem of God.

The sacred alchemy that creates trees and tree-communities, that manifests living beings and catalyzes transformation, is the great and grace-filled gift of the God of Life. How this all happens remains a beautiful mystery. Perhaps the best we can do is bear witness to the gift and tell some of our stories about what being part of this community means to us.

Our Stories

Savannah, age 45

Wilderness way is a loving spiritual family that nourishes me and helps me grow both personally and spiritually. I am reminded of my core values like compassion, tolerance, generosity, and presence. Because I experienced religious trauma as a child and because the dominant culture's version of Christianity feels oppressive to me and many others, Wilderness Way serves as a healing community where we can be our full selves and know ourselves as beloved by God and each other.

Matt G., age 42

As a lifelong social change activist rooted in the Christian faith tradition, I've found within Wilderness Way a place to belong and to be fed. Wilderness Way is a school for being alive, a support and spirituality group for people in search of our own most powerful selves—the people we were created to be.

In the context of Wilderness Way, I have grown as a person with integrity in healthy communication, as a song leader, as a scripture scholar and Liberation Bible teacher, as a person continuously invited to live my own true calling. I have been inspired over and over again by my sisters' and brothers' courage and vulnerability and enticed to live more courageously and vulnerably myself. I would not be able to carry out my own ministry without being part of Wilderness Way. I give thanks for this community!

Wilderness Way Member, age 28

Wilderness Way has been a place where I have learned and am continuing to grow my power for grounded action in the world. As someone who identifies with the experience of religious trauma, and carries multiple identities, I couldn't imagine a safer space for me to explore and be challenged to live into and discover my calling.

Wilderness Way has been a truly safe space for me to enter my grief, recharge myself for the daily work of an organizer, enter the deep wells of my own identity, and to traverse life's changes with community and hopefully a bit more grace.

I think without Wilderness Way there is a good chance I would find myself entirely outside the Christian tradition. In many ways I do, but Wilderness Way keeps challenging me to find and create liberation in the most unlikely of places. Thankfully, through Wilderness Way, I have partners in this work, and I couldn't be more grateful.

E'llee, age 9

The Wilderness Way community is so kind and loving. It has so many kind people in it and they are some of the kindest people I know. I like that they have fun stuff for the kids. And we go on hikes and walks and trails and go camping. When I am at Wilderness Way I feel happy and safe. I have lots of friends.

Instead of kneeling, standing and sitting we go on field trips, camp, explore trails and experience nature. The small community welcomes everyone. At my school you have to belong to get communion. At Wilderness Way, everyone gets communion. It is more active, we sing and dance and laugh. Everyone plays the way they want.

Nathan (former Wilderness Way member), age 32

It's not an overstatement to say that Wilderness Way was the most important and influential part of my life for five years. It was a space of deep spiritual experience, connection, and growth.

During my initial year in Portland, Wilderness Way was a new family, welcoming me into an exciting spiritual space, full of opportunities to live into the values of sabbath, jubilee, and shalom, as well as connecting me with numerous other Christian leaders in the community. As my connection to Wilderness Way grew, I was increasingly invited into leadership roles from helping to lead worship to being a part of the leadership team. Almost from the beginning, Solveig recognized my call to create music for the community and with her encouragement we now have roughly 15 songs that we use for worship.

Perhaps most importantly for me, through a combination of mentorship and invitations to leadership with partner organizations like EcoFaith Recovery and Bartimaeus Cooperative Ministries, Wilderness Way has been the catalyst for why I now feel so deeply connected to my call of youth leadership development in the context of environmental, economic, and racial justice. Words can't express my gratitude for all I have experienced in my time with Wilderness Way. If one of the hopes for a community like this is to nurture and prepare young adults for Christian leadership, I am a living testament to the powerful work of the Spirit that moves in this community.

Crystal, age 33

Finding Wilderness Way for me felt like being stranded in the middle of the ocean and then having a life boat float up to me with a bunch of amazing people saying, "We have room for you here! And lots of good food!" I grew up in fundamentalist evangelical Christianity and had a pretty good experience with the religion until my late teen years. I had a high school boyfriend I started dating at 15. By 18 we were engaged, planning to get married my sophomore year of college and determined not to have sex until then. That was hard. And I remember feeling a very distinct disconnect between the Bible and nature and thinking "This doesn't make sense." I really didn't want to get married so young. But the idea of just dating this person and not having sex for the next decade seemed ridiculous and impossible. I hated feeling pressured to get married sooner than I wanted to.

Well we did end up having sex when I was 19 and my world fell apart because I thought for sure I was going to burn forever in hell. It was really scary. Slowly more and more things made less and less sense and by 23 I was ready to put this whole Christianity thing behind me and move into the world of science and only science! I thought it would be easy to do, but I quickly learned that I couldn't just "rationalize away" extreme indoctrination.

Years and years of fear that I might be wrong about Christianity being bullshit, that I might end up in hell after all. Years and years of therapy trying to move through death anxiety and find some foundation to stand on that felt safe. I just assumed this was the only way to recover from the Christianity I had experienced and that it would just be a really long process, but that many years down the road I would finally feel at peace with dying. I even worked in the hospice field to try to catch a glimpse into my own future and see if I might find some way to face the end of my life peacefully. I remember giving voice to the most true description of the way I felt during a therapy session. I told her I felt like I was outside of a snow globe, hands and faced pressed against the glass, watching everyone else safe inside, my family, my church, heaven, God, that whole safe world just moving about peacefully without me, while I was out in the dark floating with all of the other people too stubborn to buy into the myth of Christianity and hoping they aren't wrong.

Along floats the Wilderness Way raft. I was only accustomed to a god on a cloud judging my every thought and action and writing them all down so that he can decide what to do with me when I die. I was not familiar with the Wilderness Way god, spirit, creator, divine mother, thing of many names who lives in all living things and doesn't have anything to do with sin or heaven or hell or any of the scary stuff. Wilderness Way created a new paradigm for me to think about my relationship to god. It brought me in contact with wonderful humans all with different perspectives on god, and all totally validated by Wilderness Way.

Wilderness Way was about finding all of the ways to access the spirit and saying YES! to all of them, rather than pointing out reasons why some ways weren't quite the right way for this or that theological reason. And it showed me that anyone can be a teacher or a spiritual leader. The skill is listening for the gems that we all say and think and bringing them to light. We all have so much spiritual power when we listen to one another and find our own voice. Wilderness Way wasn't inside or outside the snow globe, Wilderness Way just made it disappear all together.

I loved that Wilderness Way helped me feel more grounded, but that is only the beginning! It is amazing what I can do and what we as a community can do when we are grounded and using the skills of loving to unearth our collective spiritual power. Once I wasn't terrified every day of eternal damnation, it freed up a lot of space for me to do things that actually mattered to me and the greater world. Community organizing was something I had been doing prior to Wilderness Way but once I had this spiritual powerhouse to back me up, I had so much more energy to do all the good things. And then it felt like I was actually living the way humans were meant to live. I felt safe in my own mental space and Wilderness Way helped me feel energized and supported in whatever activist work I was doing at the time. We were all working on something, and we all supported each other's work and many of us did organizing work together.

There are a lot of ways to access the spirit and use spiritual power. I can't fight against the horrors of capitalism without my spiritual power. I'm sure a lot of people have been traumatized by religion, and people first need a safe place to work their shit out. And then they need some mentors to show them how to access and use their spiritual power. And then they need community to help amplify their power. In my experience this is the Wilderness Way. I am thankful that I have found this powerful group.

Stig, age 7

I love that Wilderness Way is a loving community and we get to play a lot and we get to access nature.

Turtle, age 32

It's hard to describe what Wilderness Way is in my life, because it has played and continues to play such a huge role. I feel really able to be myself, a person-in-process, not a shiny-polished-on version of myself. That means opportunities to express the feelings that I haven't developed as much comfort with, like grief and anger. I also have chances to push edges around things like praying out loud or leading songs, thinks that ask me to grow and stretch. What I really believe is that we are here in these bodies to learn, to grow, to take care of each other, and to take care of the Earth. (*The Blessing Seed* by Caitlin Matthews helped me find this language.) Wilderness Way really encourages putting those beliefs into practice. In this community, I feel supported to be the truest, most loving, most whole version of myself.

I like to be involved in the small parts of community life, not just the special occasions. I love spaciousness, unstructured time. Though I'm not an avid cleaner in my own space, I've had countless meaningful moments washing dishes in the homes of Wilderness Way-ers. Community is about including the unglamorous moments, about just doing life together. These micro-intimacies are my favorite. I also enjoy rituals, and am learning to expand my own day to day tool kit to include the possibility of ritual. I don't always have to do what I was scheduled to do; sometimes I need to pause and process, and that could look all kinds of ways. This is an edge I welcome.

Speaking of welcome, Wilderness Way is unusual as a Christian-identified community—ideologically broad enough for me to feel spiritually welcome and numerically small enough for me to see and be seen on a deep level.

Wilderness Way helps me keep challenging myself around sabbath, jubilee, and shalom practices. The community celebrates with me when I care for myself, when I create spaciousness in my schedule. The community listens as I describe my financial practices and constantly evolving questions around resource sharing/spending/saving, and class in general. Members of the community educate me and listen for my perspective on social and ecological justice issues, encourage my participation, and help me grapple with obstacles to engagement. When I am in conflict, within myself or with another person, I often process with another Wilderness Way-er.

Liam, age 9

Wilderness Way is a loving community where you can be yourself—animal or human or just yourself. It's a place where we sing and tell stories and make the bad feelings go away and make good feelings.

Dave, age 33

As someone who has difficulty connecting with the traditional church structure, Wilderness Way has been important for me. I appreciate the smaller, more intimate group that allows for deeper connection, and I resonate with the Wilderness motif as a lens to experience faith in the modern world. Even before coming to Wilderness Way, I have known that the values of Sabbath, Jubilee, and Shalom were crucial and often ignored in our consumptive civilization, and am glad to be sharing a journey with other folks who see this as well.

One element of Wilderness Way's rhythm that I have grown to appreciate is the practice of spiritual autobiography. Something that our pastor, Solveig, said once that has clung to my soul is that our power comes from knowing our own story, and that is why we intentionally practice the telling of our life stories. Since then, I have continued to think of the breakdown of that concept, auto-bio-graph, as the scripting of life into the bones of our selves. I have found that within the years since I landed in Portland, my life has flourished and found meaningful ways of expressing the power for transformative change that resides in my bones, and much of this is possible because Wilderness Way is a community that cultivates people who can live into their story.

Sarah, age 38

In my life, Wilderness Way has been a source of incredibly rich community, a place of honesty, silliness, and realness in sharing life deeply. I learn so much from each person, all the time—and our value of honoring the wisdom, giftedness, and sacredness of each person (and their stories) has deepened this aspect of life.

I probably would not have said yes to a formal ministry role (in the Christian church) if I were not part of a healthy, curious, courageous, deeply engaged and relevant spiritual community. Wilderness Way has helped me more strongly shape and speak my truths, particularly from the radical progressive edge of Christianity. Because of this group, I am not anxious about the decay or demise of the institutional church (or other modern US institutions). Instead, I am curious and open, trusting in Wild Spirit's new life. Being with other creative, hopeful, collaborative folk at Wilderness Way has made this possible for me. I love how we nurture grounded spiritual leadership, and how we attract healers, artists, social change agents, teachers, philosophers, entrepreneurs, and wilderness lovers of all kinds.

Shekinah, age 25

You can't have community without the intentionality to be open and honest. You can't have intentionality without real relationship, and real relationship requires vulnerability. This is what attracted me to Wilderness Way—the intentionality around vulnerability. To spend ten minutes connecting with someone before every gathering. To show up exactly as you are, and be able to express how you are. No masks, no facade. We cry AND we laugh together—because joy requires sadness. I am grateful to Wilderness Way for creating a space that allows for walls to come down and real relationships to be built. A space where I can sing about the Light or cry, cry, cry.

Peter, age 47

I have never been in a spiritual community that feels so authentic—where I could invite anyone to come and know that I wouldn't have to interpret anything, translate anything, or feel embarrassed about anything. It is one thing to have a community that means so much to me, but to have a place for our boys that is so rich, life-giving, open, and grounded in connection and story is a gift beyond imagination.

Jennilee, age 30

Wilderness Way has been a very important part of my life these past few years. I have been questioning and reevaluating my faith rather intensely. Wilderness Way has helped me to stay connected to a Christian community and become more comfortable living in this tension. I was originally fascinated by the nontraditional gathering. The language used, the practices emphasized, and the monthly rhythm have all helped me to connect with God in a way I never have before. The key to all of this, however, is the people.

Wilderness Way is led by Solveig and a group of people that warmly welcomes all who enter. The community life at Wilderness Way is more real and deep than I have yet experienced in my lifetime of church going. Vulnerability is sought and expected, but Wilderness Way also honors where everyone is in their personal journey. It is hard to describe in writing what I experience in person. You will just have to come and see.

Shelby, age 29

I am not one to believe that one should belong to a certain religion or set of beliefs. I do believe, from years of trial and error, that for me, a life based on seeking God and It's will for me is a richer, fuller life, that at times feels downright magical and that without it, life is pretty shitty. I am writing my story in hopes that it can help someone.

I came to Wilderness Way in the Late Winter of 2014. I was in a relationship with a great person, in a great apartment, and studying in a field where I got to combine my greatest passions: natural medicine, public health, social justice, eco-justice, nerdy science and woo woo earth magic. And yet, I was empty, scared I wouldn't ever be able to get myself together to actually help anyone and knew I needed help. I believed in a higher power and I had mentors who were very spiritual and even went to church. Their lives were a lot more simple and fulfilling and they were helping lots of people. I had had a rough start to life including a lot of drinking and drugs and had done a lot to clean it up. So when everything externally was going well and I still felt empty, bitter, scared, and miserable, it seemed like "a lack of faith" was my problem. So despite deep misgivings about going to a thing where people talked about Jesus, I went. I first made sure that I wouldn't have to wear a dress, that it was ok that I was a dyke, and not actually a Christian and no one was going to try to "save me." I was wary for sure.

I was told right away that the folks at Wilderness Way aren't set out to convert, that one can be rooted in a tradition while still honoring and respecting other traditions and faiths. People gave me their time and attention when I asked them about their journeys on this path. They were patient with the questions and objections I had that I bet many who have been hurt by the institutional church have. I cried a lot and felt super raw. People were loving and supportive while at the same time giving me space. It was amazing, we had super silly, don't-give-a-crap-how-ridiculous-I-look dance parties on Saturday nights and I laughed, and actually felt joy.

I loved the singing and oddly enough for me, the liberation Bible study. I loved learning stories in the Bible that actually backed up my fringy ecofeminist ideas. Issues in the Bible were being related to present day concerns like climate change, deportations, and recovery from consumerism. I met people who really drew deep inspiration and strength from Nature and Jesus and were grounded in what's going on in the world. People who were calling people in instead of calling people out, standing up to corruption, state violence, and pollution by saying, "I love you and I can't allow you to do that to us." I heard talk of symbiosis and solidarity instead of charity, how there really is enough in God's economy and in this world if only we trust God and share, and other stuff I only heard about in activist circles, not in the church I went to as a kid. And yet, the activists and organizers here were stoked about life, happy, getting shit done, and acting from a place of love and trust rather than fear and ego.

Fast forward two and a half years later, I am still walking this path. I don't yet understand why I feel called to learn about Jesus, let alone create a relationship with this fellow, but I do. Lately, when I pray to this entity, who was said to have said and done great things, I feel a stirring inside and a kind of quiet happiness and excitement, like something grand is about to happen-just-you-wait. I was a big doubter, I guess I was scared that the moment I bought into this whole thing, someone would jump out and say, "Ah ha! We fooled you! None of us actually believe in this. We just wanted to see if you were gullible, stupid and weak."

Eventually I grew tired of having my walls up and thought, "Why not? Why not just try to believe that maybe accepting help from Jesus can actually change things for me. If the worst that happens is people make fun of me, well, I think I'll be OK." I still had so many qualms with some of the content in the Bible but through Wilderness Way and then Bartimaeus Cooperative Ministries, I met so many people who were living amazing lives based on the teachings of Jesus, people who were creating change like I yearned to do but couldn't quite grasp. I met all sorts of folks who believed all sorts of things while walking a path they said Christ showed them. So I started praying to this fellow, who in my estimation, may not have even existed. I talked to the pastor about this, about why pray to someone who died. I remember she said something about energy never being destroyed. Well, perhaps, that energy, those wavelengths that he was made of are still moving and perhaps they can still be tapped into, and by tapping into those wavelengths, things within us can rearrange. I thought, OK, I can work with that. I can believe that maybe that is true, so maybe I will try this. I will pray to these wavelengths that supposedly did great things.

I was taught years ago, that if I wanted to have a life worth living, I had to start living it on a spiritual basis. And that if one wants to develop a relationship with some sort of spiritual power greater than themselves, one has to "act as if" for awhile. Just go through the motions. So about ten years ago, I spent a long time just saying prayers to the air and feeling nothing but frustration that this was supposed to help me and yet it didn't seem to be working. Eventually, things started changing, I was able to stay sober, be more patient, more kind, able to get out of unhealthy relationships, and face fears and other horribly uncomfortable feelings. I developed a working relationship with a force that I felt constituted and connected us all and moved in silent secret ways changing us in ways we couldn't do all on our own. I found that by tapping into this energetic flow, I could experience a greater peace and integrity.

So I brought this practice to considering a relationship with Jesus, who provided power to so many seeking liberation. I considered Qi, which in the acupuncture world is considered the most basic material of existence. In this way of viewing the world, where everything is made of Qi, in varying states of density, I can see how this force could have solidified itself into a state like that of a human body to move energy in very dense and material ways. And that it took very dense, material things to catch the eye of humans used to very dense material things. I still struggle with a concept of a loving God who directs things. I still struggle with the fact that there is a God that allows horrific things to occur but I am finding that spending time giving thanks alleviates some of that hurt, frustration, and confusion.

I love so much that there is room for questioning at Wilderness Way. I hope you are able to find a community that encourages you to question and seek. I feel like this process is like alchemy, it's changing iron to gold inside of me and as I keep seeking, keep reaching out—to God and to my fellows—I am further enabled to draw together my inner resources and tap into the powers that be. And with that extra strength I am slowly being transformed into a person working for systemic change that can be humble and outspoken, firm about convictions and flexible about how things unfold, persistent and loving, which I think is pretty cool, and a lot better than feeling crappy and useless.

Matt C., age 31

The complimentary themes of liberation and learning from nature kept me coming back. I just finished seminary and have been, am, and probably will continue to be critical of churches. There is no better place to be in community with other ecologically-minded, social justice-oriented, and deeply vulnerable Christians. Wilderness Way rituals help me better synthesize my ideal ethics with my actual praxis. Over the last years I have made major strides in learning from God's creation as well as refining my soul from the impurities of empire and finding love glowing in its place. Wilderness Way is really the first church that I adamantly invite friends to without reservation.

Selected Song Lyrics

OUR SONGS

We conclude this book with some of the lyrics of our favorite songs. Community singing animates our gatherings like nothing else, opening up space for Spirit to move, empowering us to find and raise our voices, creating channels of energy and connection that extend far beyond our small circle. Without the aid of microphones, screens, bulletins, or song sheets, we open our senses, listening and watching, feeling and intuiting the rhythms and melodies flowing between us. In this way, the songs sink deeply into our individual and collective consciousness, making themselves available at just the moments we need them in our daily lives or struggles for justice.

Most of our songs have been "caught" or created by members of the community. In addition to those already referenced in this book, the following are just a few of our songs that inspire us to walk the Wilderness Way.

Audio recordings of all songs printed in this book can be found on our website.

No Longer Blind

No longer blind,
Let me see, see, see
Christ in you, Christ in me!

Jesus come and heal my sight!
Help me be whole,
Let me see by your light!

By Matt Guynn

Yes! But How?

Yes, yes, yes! But how? Yes, yes, yes!
Yes, yes, yes! But how? Yes, yes, yes!

Where the Spirit's leading us now, no one knows,
But with our power and imagination,
our vision grows!

By Nathan Holst

If We Want to Move this Mountain

If we want to move this mountain,
We must move together!

Gotta make connections in the movements!
Gotta listen deeply to the other!
Gotta see our sisters and our brothers!
Gotta stop the madness with the Sabbath!
Gotta redefine how much is enough!
Gotta live shalom and know we are one!

If we want to move this mountain,
We must move together!

By Nathan Holst/Solveig Nilsen-Goodin

I'm Signing Up

I'm signing up for the Army of Peace!
I'm signing up for the Army of Hope!
I'm signing up for the Army of Justice!
I'm signing up for the Army of Love!
(Freely substitute "gospel" or "movement" for "army.")

By Matt Guynn

Spirit, Come Alive!

Spirit, come alive, let us follow the current.
Trace the sacred sighs in the call of the earth
With seven generations standing before us now.

By Nathan Holst

We are the River Rising Up

The river is flowing in us.
The river is rising with love.
We are the river, rising up!
We are the river, rising up!

The river is building us.
The river is raging with life.
We are the river, rising up!
We are the river, rising up!

By Noa Curtis and the Children of Wilderness Way

Inspired by the thousands of Standing Rock water protectors united against the Dakota Access Pipeline

Gratitude and Acknowledgments

How in the world does a small community by any measure summon the holy audacity to undertake a project such as this—collaboratively writing and publishing a book—in less than three months? Perhaps after ten wild years the stories of our community simply insisted on being shared. Or perhaps the practice of weekly calling ourselves into wildness and fearlessness rendered the absurdity of the venture irrelevant compared to the energy unleashed by the sense of call we felt. Whatever the inspiration, the combined effort and support of the entire community made this book possible.

While I drafted most of the original text, a most excellent adhoc editorial team from Wilderness Way—Amanda Bollman, Lizz Schallert, Shelby Smith, Turtle Farahat, Savannah Mayfield Roberson, Matt Guynn and Dave Pritchett—greatly improved it. Many others also offered feedback on specific sections, clarifying and improving the manuscript in significant ways. I am especially grateful to Dave Pritchett for beautifully deepening the tree metaphor with his permaculture experience. And Brittany Rasmussen and Bill Roberson's stellar proof-reading eyes caught things the rest of us missed. Thank you all!

I am grateful to Jennilee Porch for her inspiring enthusiasm getting this project started, as well as her much-needed, "We got this!" at just the moment when my energy was flagging. Amanda Bollman added a whole new dimension with her spectacular artwork, making this book as captivating to the eye as we hope it will be to the imagination. Amanda lost no small amount of sleep on this project and I am eternally grateful for her creative partnership.

And deep gratitude to Mary Nilsen of Zion Publishing for taking on the task of publishing a community writing project with all the chaos, delays, last-minute testimony submissions and changes that brings. Thank you for bringing your expertise, unflagging support and unending grace to this creative collaboration.

Beyond that, the voices of our members provide the depth and breadth of the Wilderness Way experience to enrich and animate this book. Thank you to all who found the courage to put your experience into words.

Wilderness Way has evolved and matured through the participation of so many—some who sojourned with us for a year, a few months, or even a few weeks. But Wilderness Way simply would not exist were it not for three groups of people. First and foremost, I give thanks for the current community of Wilderness Way. You are some of the most spectacular people I know, each searching, stretching, transforming in community and as community. Walking (stumbling, crawling, dancing) the Way with you humbles and emboldens me. I am wilder and braver because of you, my faith freer and fiercer because of you. Thank you for being manna for me.

Before the current community there was the group of six: Matt Guynn, Sarah Kinsel, Turtle Farahat, Nathan Holst, and Peter Nilsen-Goodin who, along with myself, still felt called into community when others found their own paths. Together we listened endlessly (at least it felt endless!) for the essence of Wilderness Way, singing over and over again, "Yes! But How?" —one of the many treasured songs Nathan gifted to the community. Without you the tender young sapling of Wilderness Way would never have matured as it has.

And before the group of six there was the original group of nine: Mark Douglass, Betsy Branch, Dale Stitt, Esther Elizabeth, Scott, Ladine and Evan Marquardt, Peter and myself, along with two little ones at the time, Scottie and Soren.

This original group of people risked putting their trust, time, energy and resources into this thing we called Wilderness Way. Your willingness to pour your lives into a wild experiment humbles me still. Without you the seed of Wilderness Way would never have taken root.

And finally, at the very beginning, there was my friend and long-time creative collaborator, Mark Douglass, who dared to share a vision with me one day as we sipped tea on the couch in my living room. Like John leaping inside Elizabeth's womb, when I heard Mark's vision of an alternative church, something within me leapt, and the course of my life changed forever. If I were to dedicate this book to any one person it would be you, Mark. Co-nurturing this vision/seed with you in those early years was an extraordinary experience, and everyone who has ever been or ever will be touched by Wilderness Way owes you a debt of gratitude—gratitude to you for heeding that still small voice that whispered, "I am about to do a new thing; now it springs forth, do you not perceive it? I will make a way in the wilderness..." (Isaiah 43:19). Thank you, Mark.

And most of all I give thanks to the irrepressible and irresistible God of Life. Untamable yet utterly trustworthy, this wild, divine Wisdom relentlessly and lovingly coaxes me to loosen my grip on anything I try to control, and graciously reveals to me over and over again that indeed, everything I need is right in front of me.

"Where the Spirit's leading us now, no one knows! But with our power and imagination, our vision grows!" May the words of Nathan's song and the stories in this book inspire all of us to walk the Wilderness Way and manifest in our own time and place the beloved Ecosystem of God.

HOW TO CONNECT

Website: www.wildernesswaypdx.org
Email: wildernesswaycommunity@gmail.com
Facebook: Wilderness Way

Weekly gatherings (at the time of this printing)
Sundays 3:00—5:30 p.m.

LEAVEN COMMUNITY CENTER
5431 NE 20th Ave
Portland, OR 97211

Note: On the 3rd Sundays of each month we take our
Sabbath walk in the woods, followed by a potluck.
Locations vary. Email if you would like to join us!

Made in the USA
Charleston, SC
13 October 2016